WINNIPEG
JAN 04 2017
PUBLIC LIBRARY

questions i asked my mother

D0891354

WINNIPEG

JAN 0 4 2017

PUBLIC LIBRARY

questions i asked my mother

✧

di brandt

afterword by Tanis MacDonald

TURNSTONE PRESS

questions i asked my mother
copyright © Di Brandt 1987
revised edition, 2015

Turnstone Press
Artspace Building
206-100 Arthur Street
Winnipeg, MB
R3B 1H3 Canada
www.TurnstonePress.com

All rights reserved. No part of this book may be reproduced or transmitted in any form or by any means—graphic, electronic or mechanical—without the prior written permission of the publisher. Any request to photocopy any part of this book shall be directed in writing to Access Copyright, Toronto.

Published in Canada by Turnstone Press in 2015. First published in Canada by Turnstone Press in 1987.

Turnstone Press gratefully acknowledges the assistance of the Canada Council for the Arts, the Manitoba Arts Council, the Government of Canada through the Canada Book Fund, and the Province of Manitoba through the Book Publishing Tax Credit and the Book Publisher Marketing Assistance Program.

The epigraph on page ix has been excerpted from *Stranger Music* by Leonard Cohen. Copyright © 1993 Leonard Cohen. Reprinted by permission of McClelland & Stewart, a division of Penguin Random House Canada Limited.

Some of these poems and stories appeared previously in *Northern Light, Border Crossings, Contemporary Verse 2, The New Quarterly, CMBC Alumni Bulletin, The Mennonite Mirror, The Dinosaur Review, Prairie Fire,* and *Esther Warkov: Recent Drawings.*

Printed and bound in Canada by Friesens for Turnstone Press.

Library and Archives Canada Cataloguing in Publication
Brandt, Di, author
        Questions I asked my mother / Di Brandt ; afterword by Tanis MacDonald.

Poems.
Includes bibliographical references.
ISBN 978-0-88801-505-1 (paperback)

        I. Title.

PS8553.R2953Q4 2015   C811'.54   C2015-903766-2

in loving memory of my mother Mary

with thanks to the many readers around the world
who have made this book a more beautiful adventure
than i could ever have imagined

some of this is autobiographical & some of it is not

If I have been untrue
I hope you know it was never to you
—Leonard Cohen

foreword

learning to speak *in public*   to write love poems
for all the world to read   meant betraying once &
for all the good Mennonite daughter i tried so
unsuccessfully to become   acknowledging in myself
the rebel traitor thief   the one who asked too
many questions   who argued with the father & with
God   who always took things always went too far
who questioned every thing   the one who talked too
often too loud   the questionable one   shouting
from rooftops what should only be thought guiltily
in secret   squandering stealing the family words
the one out of line   recognizing finding myself
in exile   where i had always been   trying as
always to be true   whispering in pain the old
words   trying to speak the truth as it was given
listening in so many languages & hearing in this one
translating   remembering   claiming my past
living my inheritance on this black earth   among
strangers   prodigally   making love in a foreign
country   writing coming home

contents

foreword / xi

1. shades of sin

when i was five / 3
Marian makes lists / 4
but what do you think / 5
questions i asked my mother / 6
shades of sin / 9
say to yourself each time / 13
ruling his shrunken kingdom / 14
legs astride arms akimbo / 15
my mother found herself / 16
Diana / 17

2. always this other person

I sing the Rubber Lady / 23
bathroom poems / 24
she lost perspective they said / 29
always this other person / 30
missionary positions / 31
testimony / 38
every word to you / 39
you want to hear what it was like / 40
at least they left you arms & legs / 41
valentine / 42

3. & i what do i want

last night i slept with a clown / 45
paraphernalia for a love scene / 46
valkyrie song / 47
in your paintings / 48
& i what do i want / 49
i hate desire / 50
i will dance mighty ones / 51
it's a talent loving old men / 52
the year he was dying / 53
the grandfathers she said / 54

4. hear them whispering

i wish the sky was still pasted on / 57
mother why didn't you tell me this / 58
trying to climb / 59
how come there were all those stories / 60
hear them whispering / 61
who would have thought / 62
i wanted so much to be / 63
you think if you say the right words / 64
because she is not here / 65
seeing the world feelingly / 66
i want you to know / 67

looking forward looking back / 69

Thirty Years of Questions: An Afterword to Di Brandt's
questions i asked my mother by Tanis MacDonald / 71

1. shades of sin

when i was five i thought heaven was located
in the hayloft of our barn the ladder to get
up there was straight & narrow like the Bible
said if you fell off you might land on the
horns of a cow or be smashed on cement the men
in the family could leap up in seconds wielding
pitchforks my mother never even tried for us
children it was hard labour i was the scaredy
i couldn't reach the first rung so i stood at the
bottom & imagined what heaven was like there
was my grandfather with his Santa Claus beard
sitting on a wooden throne among straw bales
never saying a word but smiling & patting us
on the head & handing out bubble gum to those
who were good even though his eyes were half
closed he could see right inside your head so
i squirmed my way to the back of the line &
unwished the little white lie i had told which
i could feel growing grimy up there & tried
not to look at the dark gaping hole where they
shoved out black sinners like me but the best
part was the smell of new pitched hay wafting
about some of it fell to where i stood under
the ladder there were tiny blue flowerets pressed
on dry stems i held them to my nose & breathed
deep sky & sun it was enough heaven for me for
one day

Marian makes lists of all the things she doesn't
want to forget what groceries to buy chores to be
done by the end of the week people's birthdays so
she can send them cards from the Regal collection
with the cute kittens on the box the cost of nails
hammer paintbrushes turpentine scrapers wallpaper
for the spare bedroom so she can keep track me
i carry around this list of things i can't forgive
the time my mother made me stand in the corner
by the basement steps & my cousin Joyce came
over & i had to pretend i was so engrossed in
Reader's Digest i wasn't the slightest bit interested
in going bike riding with her & the sun shining first
time in a week or the time my sister got sucked
into raising her hand at evangelical meeting & she
had to get counselling from the deacon behind the
coat rack after church or my brother pulling the
wings off sparrows & swinging the cat by its tail
just to make us scream & my mother always thinking
he was a saint & my dad grotesquely cheerful after
milking barging into the room with his grin & good
morning & we with our awkward limbs only half
dressed oh yes like Marian i remember my family
i tally up prices i keep track

≈

but what do you think my father says this verse means if it's not
about the end of the world look that's obviously a misreading i say
the verb grammatically speaking doesn't have an object in this
instance so it can't possibly be made to that's exactly what i mean
he says waving the book in mid air if my father ever shouted he
would be shouting now you don't really care about the meaning all
you ever think about is grammar & fancy words i never even heard
of where i come from the reason you learn to read is to understand
God's Holy Word i only went to school 7 year & it's done me okay
what are you going to do with all this hifalutin education anyway
don't you think it's time you got a job & did some honest work for
a change the meaning i say through clenched teeth is related to the
structure of the sentence for godsake anybody can see that you can't
just take some old crackpot idea & say you found it in these words
even the Bible has to make some sense the Bible my father says
the veins in his neck turning a slow purple is revealed to those
gathered together in His name you don't even go to church how
can you know anything of the truth you're no better than the heathen
on the street the way you live around here if i'd aknown my own
daughter would end up like this you're the one i say who started this
conversation what did you ask me for if i'm not entitled to an opinion
please my mother says crying as usual why don't we go for a walk
or something you think i'll weep i'll not weep we glare at each other
with bright fierce eyes my father & i she still tries after all these years
to end this argument between us arrest deflect its bitter motion does
she know this is all there is for us these words dancing painfully across
the sharp etched lines of his God ridden book & does she does he
do we really want this crazy cakewalk to stop

5

questions i asked my mother

look when grampa died last week everybody said he's better off
where he is because he's in heaven now he's with God we should
be happy he's gone home but yesterday when they put him in the
ground the minister said he's going to be there till the last trumpet
raises the quick & the dead for the final judgement now look
mom i can't figure out which is true it's got to be either up or
down i mean what's he gonna do swoop back into his body at the
last moment so he can rise with the trumpet call or what i got to
know mom what do you think   my mother is sewing she's
incredibly nimble with her fingers my father marvels at them she's
sewed all our clothes since we were born embroidered designed
them   she bites the thread carefully before answering   now
Diana she says & then stops   i can see my question is too
much for her   Dad she calls into the other room come here a
minute & listen to what this girl is asking   i have to repeat the
whole thing my voice rising desperately   well when grampa
died last week everybody said he's better off where he is because
he's in heaven now he's with God but yesterday when they put
him in the ground the minister said he's going to be there till the
last trumpet raises the quick & the dead for the final judgement &
i can't figure out which is true he's got to be either up or down
what's he gonna do swoop back into his body at the last moment
so he can rise with the trumpet call or what   they look at
each other complicity in their eyes   i don't think that's a very
nice thing to say about grampa she begins   she wouldn't say
this if we were alone it's an introduction   she lets him finish
with the big stuff   it's your attitude he says i've noticed lately
everything you say has this questioning tone i don't think you're
really interested in grampa or your faith what you really want is to

6

make trouble for mom & me you've always been like that you're
always trying to figure everything out your own way instead of
submitting quietly to the teachings of the church when are you
going to learn not everything has to make sense your brain is not
the most important thing in the world what counts is your attitude
& your faith your willingness to accept the mystery of God's
ways   another time i asked her mom   i been thinking about
arithmetic & what i'm wondering is do you think arithmetic was
invented or discovered i mean it seems like it must have been
invented because all these signs numbers & things they didn't find
those lying on a rock somewhere people must have made them
up but on the other hand it really works i mean do you think
anybody could have invented 10 times 10 is a hundred & if so
who could it have been   well i just don't know she says
wonderingly i've never really thought about it you sure come up
with the strangest questions really i don't know how you got to be
so smart   sometimes i just felt i would burst with all the
unanswered questions inside me i thought of writing the *Country
Guide* question & answer column but i didn't have stationery &
anyway no one ever asked questions like that   i imagined
heaven as a huge schoolroom where all the questions of the
universe were answered once & for all God was the cosmic school
inspector pointing eternally to a chalkboard as big as the sky
just imagine i thought Abraham & Isaac & all those guys they
already know everything they knew about relativity centuries before
Einstein instantly like that they don't ever have to think   one
time i asked her about bread   i loved smelling the brown yeast
in the huge blue speckled bowl its sweetish ferment watching it
bubble & churn how does it turn into bread i asked her   well

the yeast is what makes it rise she said when you add warm water
it grows as you can see yes but how does it turn into bread i
mean it comes out a completely different thing what exactly
happens to it in there in the oven why does heat turn it into
something full of holes we can eat   she sighed my mother
sighed a lot when i was around   you're asking me something
i can't tell you she said now help me punch down the dough
i sat in front of the oven all afternoon bathed in warm kitchen
smells trying to figure it out someday i said to myself someday
i will find out i will find out everything

shades of sin

the temptations of men in Reinland were blatant contemptible
easily accomplished & thrown away cigarettes at Yurchak's Sunday
afternoons ancient dust curled calendar pictures of half naked
women the grey foreign monotony of tv on a tiny corner shelf
for the women sin came much better disguised subtle attractive
creeping into every day pride for example the everlurking
temptation to think you were somebody hold your head up too
straight on the street or in church or forget yourself so far as to
speak your own mind   it happened to the best of women once
in a while though in my family at least they made up for it after
with extra baking & sweet talk for weeks   the big one for Rosie
& me was glamour an obviously forbidden kind of worldliness but
with peculiarly undefined edges a lot of our adolescent energies
went into their exact location the rules kept changing that was the
confusing part   we could understand for example that hair was
an unruly item best kept under kerchiefs & hats its dangerous
tendency to shine in the sun & spring provocative curls
sometimes without prompting   we liked to cite nature as
justification though the most unsophisticated theologian among us
could veto this claim easily with reference to the Fall   the point
was partly to protect ourselves against the brutal demands of
men whose biological urges unlike our own could not be helped it
was therefore up to us to keep them from getting unduly aroused
but mainly we suspected to do with the thing itself   beauty was
altogether a disturbing category for Mennonites no one knew quite
what to do with it even though God must have put it there for a
reason if we could only know what it was   & yet our mothers
dared to disobey their own fathers' decrees so far as to cut & curl
their hair even administering the occasional home permanent to

each other & sometimes us children that was okay though looking
in the mirror longer than say thirty seconds at a time or admitting
any pleasure whatsoever in the results was strictly taboo as
ever   the hats themselves were fraught with temptation
according to the Bible women had to cover their hair for worship
a handy excuse for keeping one's Sunday headwear up to date
though one of my aunts insisted it meant 100% cotton
handkerchiefs from Gladstone's tied around the chin   my
mother ordered her hats from Eaton's by mail she favoured a
pleasant middle of the road style neither too rakish nor too plain
light beige navy blue with a modest bit of lace once they sent her
a thin black hat with a net veil to cover the face we loved this hat
its dangerous mystique   she wouldn't wear it until she figured
out a way to tuck the veil in so it looked only an inch long that
was what bothered me most of all the clearcut invisible lines of
propriety which could not be argued or discussed & seemed
obvious to everyone except Rosie & me   it just didn't make
sense a necklace was acceptable to God up to say two strands if
the beads were not too large or too brightly coloured but the
tiniest bracelet plunged you immediately over into heathenism
someone who could it have been gave my mother a set of fake
diamonds once she wore the necklace to church with her
embroidered blue checked cotton dress but the earrings stayed on
her dresser in a little case we longed for these earrings fondled
them screwed them secretly in our ears   she let us wear them
sometimes for dressup but we had to be careful not to look
exuberant or glamorous a hard thing when you're eight & wearing
diamonds or my dad would threaten to take them away to chasten
our pride   she had several items like this a pair of white satin

gloves the long kind that reached past the elbow & featured a slit
at the wrist to tuck in the hand part if you were at a ball & sitting
down to dinner   a pair of red leather shoes with open toes &
three inch heels never worn   a pair of short pink gloves with
white pearls sewn at the wrist   how did these things come to
be in Reinland   when asked she would smile vaguely &
murmur something about changing her mind   when i was ten
a group of village mothers organized a 4H tour to Winnipeg for
their children   we left at seven in the morning by bus   Rosie & i
were wearing blue pedal pushers our mother whipped up late the
night before on the Singer sewing machine   our first stop was
CKY i can't for the life of me imagine how such a worldly radio
station got on the agenda since we weren't allowed to listen to
anything but CFAM in Reinland   i don't remember anything
about the tour itself except the lady who showed us around she
was the most glamorous person we had ever laid our innocent
eyes on   we feasted on her gloriously wicked appearance all up
& down the halls of the CKY building from her dubiously spiked
grey leather heels to her blue shaded eyelids   the best thing
by far was her bracelet a silver chain hung with we could hardly
believe it dimes there must have been hundreds of them rattling
& jingling as she talked   we spent half the trip home later
discussing this fascinating item calculating its worth its glitter
its sinfulness its waste   our second stop was the Christie cookie
factory our mothers were more at home here & more relaxed
we watched thousands of tiny rectangle biscuits slipping off
conveyor belts & being stuck together with lemon yellow icing
impressive but most of us agreed the results fell far short of the
baking we were used to at home   our third stop was the

Museum after lunch someone decided we should split into smaller
groups to walk through it since there was no tour guide we would
be on our own   Rosie & i stayed with our mother we made
a great mistake walking into the Museum our group somehow we
made a wrong turn & ended up in the Art Gallery on the other
side   i don't know what we would have seen in the Museum
had we ever found it but what we saw instead was mind boggling
nothing pretty or picturesque like the calendars at home only
weird smudges which gave you a strange feeling in the belly
my mother embarrassed & sweaty about the mistake hurried us
through them still hoping for stuffed buffaloes & red coats on
wooden mannikins somewhere but she only led us deeper into
the labyrinth of Art   the most incredible room of all was the
very last hung all around with naked women in various poses
our first glimpse of the shape our own bodies were destined
to become   i would have liked to stay in this room awhile &
sort out the strange emotions aroused by this totally new vision
of the world but for the sake of our education we rushed on &
made it out just as the last of the other groups emerged from the
Museum so easily located after all just across the big hall   my
mother of course turned the whole adventure into an episode in
getting lost sorting through inch by inch the wrong turns we
had made our good fortune in getting out at all   she never
mentioned the room full of naked women & neither did we
there didn't seem to be any words for it but it stayed in my memory
as a kind of promise touching some deeper hunger than i had
known untouched by more familiar shades of sin

say to yourself each time lips vagina tongue
lips do not exist catch the rising sob in
your throat where it starts deep under your
belly the tips of your breasts your secret
flowing your fierce wanting & knowing say
to yourself the ache in your thighs your big
head full of lies your great empty nothing
despise despise the Word of God is the Word
of God sit still stop your breathing look
down at your numb legs your false skirt sighing
sit still & listen

ruling his shrunken kingdom from a wheelchair
my father peels potatoes in his withered
women's lap his forty years dominion over
every living thing comes only to this playing
cook's helper in my mother's kitchen his
mighty furrowed thousand acres contracted so
suddenly to her modest garden plot we are
made breathless by this hasty engagement
the shocking imprudence of a sick man's match
it isn't so far from what he would have wished
sitting in the sun on his mother's ancient
weathered wooden bench thinking old men's
thoughts & yet he holds through this indecent
bedding down to the lawful words of his old
command & she continues to obey while under
our desperate family charade his thick fingers
fumblingly caress these earth brown globes
learning gropingly to say the silent love words
of his abdicating

෨

legs astride   arms akimbo
my father tilts his cap back
mops his black forehead
    leaving streaks of sweat
    on wet   glistening skin

his teeth when he laughs
    are incredibly white
    the inside of his lips bright red
later when he washes off the grain dust
    i will see the line between
    his smooth white biceps
    & the red brown leather
    of his arms

he carried me once
across this golden field
    on his shoulders
the stubble had scratched a thousand
    red welts in my skin
the swathe was too wide to jump
anyway

our shadow stretched across
    two rows of ripe cut wheat
the ft ft ft of his lithesome feet
measured the red gold of the burning
    sun across the long
    distance of my yearning

15

my mother found herself one late summer
afternoon lying in grass under the wild
yellow plum tree jewelled with sunlight
she was forgotten there in spring picking
rhubarb for pie & the children home from
school hungry & her new dress half hemmed
for Sunday the wind & rain made her skin
ruddy like a peach her hair was covered
with wet fallen crab apple blossoms she
didn't know what to do with her so she put
her up in the pantry among glass jars of
jellied fruit she might have stayed there
all winter except we were playing robbers
& the pantry was jail & every caught thief
of us heard her soft moan she made her
escape while we argued over who broke the
pickled watermelon jar scattering cubes
of pale pink flesh in vinegar over the
basement floor my mother didn't mind she
handed us mop & broom smiling & went back
upstairs i think she was listening to
herself in the wind singing

Diana

i used to have a lot of trouble with my name   in Reinland
where i grew up people named their children Peter & Agnes &
Sara & Jacob   in fact there was so much duplication of names
you might find yourself in the position of say Peter Peters son
of Peter Peters son of Peter Peters   this wasn't as confusing as
it sounds   there wasn't a lot of mail & the identities of fathers
& sons were not that clearly distinguished anyway   most of the
time you referred to people by their nicknames which everybody
knew like Schwauta Petasch or Boaut Jaunzen   what was an
exotic name like Diana doing in a plain village like Reinland
not only did it lack the resonance of a long line of aunts &
grandmothers it was hard for people to say   they would roll it
around on their tongues tasting its foreignness & then spit it out
a friend of my grandfather's once asked me aren't you terribly
depressed to have a name like that   my mother's cousin Susch
was undaunted by it   she would hug me tight on her lap &
tickle & squeeze me with her crippled hand all the while crooning
Diantche oba Diantche oba Diantche   later my brother & sister
would follow me around mercilessly chanting Diantche oba
Diantche   part of the joke was it sounded a lot like little
duckling little duckling in Low German   we didn't get to read
books much   the school library was a tiny cupboard in the
corner of the room   you could read through the entire
collection in half a year & you only got to switch rooms every four
years   the public library which came to town once a month in
a van was forbidden to us on grounds of worldliness   but we did
get to hear a fantastic array of Bible stories   i was fascinated by
their exotic foreign flavour   they always came with a moral
attached at the end which would relate them to our own plain

little world but it never came close to capturing their beauty &
terror   it was extremely hard to see for example how the point
of a story like the multicoloured Joseph in Egypt being seduced
by Potiphar's wife could possibly be that we shouldn't tell lies to
our parents   i did find one story which i felt i could claim for
my own   my second name is Ruth so i paid particular attention
to Ruth the Moabite who followed her mother in law home &
worked in the fields with her   her faithfulness made her belong
in spite of her foreign past   your people shall be my people &
your God shall be my God   i clung to this story as a way of
getting through the other passage from the Bible which had to do
with me   whenever the minister in church read about the
heathenish Diana of the Ephesians & the wickedness she caused
among God's people i modestly lowered my head & tried to look
Ruthlike   i even told my teacher once to call me Ruth from now
on   she smiled indulgently & instantly forgot   later   in high
school i discovered other more interesting stories about the
goddess whose name i bore   Greek myths were okay to read
as long as you didn't mix them up with the Bible   they were
strictly classical references to explain the strange names strewn so
improvidently through English literature which we had to read to
get through Grade 12   i found out that she was a huntress &
a moon goddess both of which suited me fine   there weren't
any forests around our farm but i could easily imagine gliding
among trees in buskins & i was on intimate terms with the moon
already   a ghostly galleon tossed upon cloudy seas   she was
also the virgin goddess which worried me a lot during the time my
twin sister Rosie & her friends were going on heavy dates & i was
sitting at home vascillating between the terror of acquiring breasts

& periods & the shame of getting them so late   i liked the story
of Actaeon who was turned into a stag for spying on Diana   it
was a thrill to think of being able to turn boys' tricks inside out like
that   by this time my friends were calling me Di which i liked
because it was short & neat & it turned every greeting into a little
song   hi Di bye Di   the only problem with it was meeting
new people who would usually raise their eyebrows & say oh you
mean Diane & even if i emphasized the *a* at the end of Diana they
would still invariably spell it with a double *n* or some other
unforgivable mistake   this problem was solved miraculously
forme a few years ago by his royal highness Prince Charles   he
couldn't know of course that his choice of the future Queen of
England would personally affect the identity of a missing Mennonite
peasant girl from Reinland   but it did   since the advent
of Lady Di no one has ever questioned my name   in fact
it has given me my own modest taste of royalty   a five year
old girl at Victoria Albert school in Winnipeg came up to me one
day & said i saw you on tv   what was i doing on tv i asked her
much surprised   getting married she said   to Prince
Charles   so i felt like a princess for one day   going back to
Reinland now i notice several young Dianas swinging in the school
yard & skipping in the ditches   nothing feels as separate as
everything once did   it's hard to tell anymore what is exotic &
what is plain   i like it that way

2. always this other person

I sing the Rubber Lady
        varicosed
        garter hosed
her inflatable elastic self
ballooning today in high wind
on the string of veined promises
you may pop her with a prick
if you can hold her long enough
I sing the silver gashed stretch marks
on her eight month belly
gulping in greedily large draughts
of rarified electric air
her hair is becoming rooted
in storm clouds
her breath the snorting
of wild horses
bring her down with a needle
sharply
but do it with rubber gloves
this lady is high voltage

bathroom poems

1

searching for my self in various ladies
i have subscribed to endless circulars
proclaiming us blood kin in these rooms
i have rolled & unrolled with the rest
wordless sheets announcing the damp odour
of our common text like you i have avoided
all eyes in this crowded mirror except my
own waiting for a reissue of the lost

2

unlike the woman in fur who found her
country's jet hole too small & got
caught by her own fetus refusing to
shrink the drain in my bathroom sink
is so big i have lost all my thin legged
babies in slippery water i have tried
everything less soap rubber gloves a new
plumber the next one stays unwashed

3

there's a black bear under the stairs
he whispers robbers hiding behind the
furnace didn't you know i manage to
hold out until dark a stupid tactic
i realize too late & descend with numb
legs to the necessary pit remembering
his grin i stare wide eyed into every
dark corner but they are playing hide
& seek with me i catch only a faint
whiff of june berries & the dull clink
of gold on burlap as i leave

4

in my dreams i walk down long
exitless corridors find myself
in barred hospital rooms swim
hopelessly against the motion
of black conveyor belts knock
on twelve inch doors please i
gotto go real bad getting past
the frowning fat lady & her
greasy nickels is the easy part
you can fool her with a pebble
if she's not looking the clink
in her dish all she cares about
it's them miniature elephants
in the windows with the glinting
rubied eyes i'm worried over
not sure how big they get or when
the key melts in my hand inside
the door a loud alarm shatters
the world into day the bathroom's
a dozen ordinary steps across
an empty hall

5

behind the tame graffiti on these blue
shining walls Thriftee Snowite Sanitation
i remember in the corner by the door
under the yellow spotted spider's web
green apple scented tissues Eaton's dresses
with foreign frills the forbidden rainbow
coloured thrill of the Katzenjammer kids

she lost perspective they said at
first skipping the occasional beat
then they noticed entire bars missing
finally the score itself blank space
still she refused to stop humming
soft lyrics a caress & even sometimes
a wild shout without words mind you
all this without focus having lost
as they said direction the converging
point you can't make music without
fixing the horizon straight lines
at least no meaning without measure

❧

always this other person beside me dog voice yapping
at the heel shut up won't you for once companion in the
night sometimes a second opinion yes but a stranger's
who are you anyway

looking into the flames they saw three figures walking
unharmed god spelled backwards that's you officials
having revised the figures on the number of dead news
men's prerogative me always the listener listen i want
to be the one talking not yaps grunts beeps not the
latest update but remembering something i can't remember
something about a dog

missionary position (1)

let me tell you what it's like
having God for a father & jesus
for a lover on this old mother
earth you who no longer know
the old story the part about the
Virgin being of course a myth
made up by Catholics for an easy
way out it's not that easy i can
tell you right off the old man
in his room demands bloody hard
work he with his rod & his hard
crooked staff well jesus he's
different he's a good enough lay
it's just that he prefers miracles
to fishing & sometimes i get tired
waiting all day for his bit of
magic though late at night i burn
with his fire & the old mother
shudders & quakes under us when
God's not looking

missionary position (2)

there was a great crashing in my
ears the day God became man & the
last heavy link of the great command
came tumbling to earth i became my
own mother that sunlit morning on
the rose faded carpet i swallowed
her bird cries her deep granite
frown i took the great godman into
my belly unchained we savoured each
hot whispered word made flesh we
mouthed our slow pleasure in long
grass dizzied along the blood earth's
singing

missionary position (3)

or i could talk about the thousand
burnt offerings which never reached
heaven smoke drifting sideways always
blown back in my eyes fierce grunting
& groaning all night & never a blessing
only crippled thighs & never forgiveness
for the missing silver cup the sun moon
& stars forever unbending clay in the
sky the seasons sour in the belly my
limbs heavy with aching still wanting
you

missionary position (4)

these things are really true
Mary is my mother & her favourite
colour is blue my grandfather
Peter was a firm believer &
founded a church she is gentle
meek & mild & proud as a queen
he was stubborn as a rock &
stone deaf in one ear growing
up between them was like living
between earth & sky watching the
woolly lambs of heaven watching
him die early on Easter morning
she wept at his grave & we played
in the grass we danced barefoot
until sundown like naked strangers
in a field

missionary position (5)

of all the virgins that last summer
heidi you & i we were the wisest
how we strutted down empty streets
lamps nearly bursting not spilling
a drop how we dreamed of our bride
groom the shadowy prince disdaining
boys' touches oh we knew what we
wanted not for us to be caught with
our pants down & oil running out
not with heaven beckoning us no sir
how we smirked at the foolish ones
burning their capital after dark
behind closed shops how we gloated
over our own saving we waited wise
virgins that long summer to be swept
into clouds we wandered fires unlit
to its end

missionary position (6)

it's hard to choose among my dozen
lovers any one king they're all
charming in their way each one is
different of course one always
hard as a rock another soft like
a mother they like to do different
things one talks all the time the
next never says a word one never
stops telling me how beautiful i
am i like that another gets straight
down to business & that's that one
of them fancies strange places steep
riverbanks clover in ditches another
takes photographs & hangs me in
kitchens one prefers holding another
kissing one looks deep into my eyes
one tells me only lies i don't know
each one makes me feel like a queen
if i had to choose between them but
i don't thank God he made twelve a
good number for mates

just kidding   ma

testimony

they shake their heads in disbelief
but it's true i found jesus at last
i took him into my heart & he brought
me deep joy he was the world's greatest
lover he was so gentle & rough his
lips & his tongue & his soft hairy
belly his thighs & the nakedness of
his soft hard cock he filled up my
aching my dark gaping void he wiped
the tears from my unseeing eyes oh
yes i was lost & then i was found
while the dew was still on the roses
in the arms of my precious jewelled
lord i'm saved brothers & sisters
jesus saved me

every word to you betrays the old
father & his wives their greedy
hungry eyes their mouths full of
stones i never meant to leave them
always tried to be good & here in
this capturing far away like always
they surround me the old old circle
no matter what i say where i go i
see them crouching waiting impatient
for my last false move

you want to hear what it was like she says
growing up with you no one ever asked me
what i thought about anything they just
wanted to know about you why you said things
what you wanted what do you think i was
doing all those years while you were busy
arguing so stupid & stubborn with Dad do you
know we always played your favourite games
read your books bought your favourite purses
do you know how hard i tried to act & walk
& look like you did you ever once think how
i felt being the short one the dark one
people forgetting i was born first oh sure
the athletic one out playing with boys you
know as well as i do what that was worth
you know what i thought when we prayed in
the living room on Sundays God doesn't hear
me he's reading his damn book again turning
the pages too fast like she does do you know
how much i wanted to be like you how much i
wanted to be you have you any idea she says
how much i loved you

at least they left you arms & legs
Rose Red think what it was like with
only a fucking head not much room
for sliding around bases catching
balls you call them fortrel princes
now the losers taking what they could
get with you the leavings think what
it was like for me floating inside
the old glass bubble gulping my own
words desperately for air i saw those
guys with their strange offerings
their clumsy slow pitches i didn't
have arms Rosy never mind your fancy
fitted gloves the reason i held my
head up so high was they cut off my
legs dreaming crystal i didn't have
knees

valentine

i wish i could fasten her edges
one by one with my mouthful of
head pins stand her in the corner
at right angles back against the
wall like paper dolls measure her
shoulders her ankles her frown
hold her at arm's length just once
i wish i could make her could make
my mother love me

3. & i what do i want

last night i slept with a clown with a wide
foolish grin & big ears i could see from his
tricks & his rags he was a gypsy & a juggler
& i know from his crooked crown he was also
jesus & he was you & once in a while when he
talked he was my father & the wonder of it was
he was laughing himself crazy over something
i said he was the answer to all husbands &
lovers he tossed me so lightly with his quick
hands into the place of my deceiving there was
no coming down nothing to pay until the
morning

paraphernalia for a love scene

(paraphernalia: "those articles of personal
property which the law allowed a married
woman to keep and, to a certain extent, deal
with as her own" —OED)

i will bring feathers & fishbones from old
summer beaches i will scratch out my name
on your back with black ink we will dance
on the shards of dead Indians & sing with
beetles you will not have to say the words
that kill you i will do everything & after
the old naked fisherman has walked by we will
lie in his green boat & count pelicans in
the green bay i will crown your hair with
poison ivy cover your limbs with white sand
you will not be denied your final ecstasy

valkyrie song

like usual he's got it all wrong men
no matter what you tell them always
think with the end of their dink well
how can i help it he says waving it
wildly in air wouldn't you too if you
had one down there listen there's more
than one story in the world remember
the old woman with the wild toothless
grin rattling her coins before dropping
them in the fox in the stable with the
flaming red tail not finding the chickens
in the milk pail for once can't you stop
thinking about cutting it off or sticking
it in or making it grow it's making me
nervous you know what i want she says
turning her face to the wall is your
children or better yet nothing at all
once in a snowstorm under a tree that's
where i had him & he had me we burned
up the blizzard with our hot tongues
& fed the dark pain in us belly deep
what i want she says opening her
liquidy eyes is your dark arms around
me so i can cry

❧
(for Les)

in your paintings i am almost always
looking away while your brush so easily
imagines my thighs dreams apricot bellies
ankles breasts the delicate contour of
nipples you're so good at i am looking
away into distant nonexistent horizons
i am reading *Paradise Lost* listening for
cries of birds & sleeping children i am
thinking veiled thoughts of secret lovers
i am asleep i am waiting always for the
soft invisible stroke of your brilliant
caress

♋

& i what do i want in this my contradictory
most treacherous false heart of hearts
i want you passionate steed sword & bridle
gleaming the hero still to carry me away
with your longing capture me in your flaming
eternal all knowing yes in spite of everything
the women the teacups the wine sitting together
here in this room speaking our independence
our new vision what i want is the old promises
all the ironies swept away Cinderella rising
from the ashes glassy eyed her empty face
her transparent shoes

≪⧽

i hate desire the hot animal itch
of it yours & mine in every thing
waking or sleeping i can't even
walk down the street without this
lust this ache this fever stretching
between us scratching my eyes my
belly my thighs i wish i'd never
had you inside me come with you
in that place full of hurt i wish
there was love without this great
wanting this huge empty tear in the
chest

i will dance mighty ones i will dance
on your brittle bones i will eat your
old glowing between the shadows of the
Almighty's knowing & the sun's daily
glitter i will string together such
words though they are made of earth
they shall be the world's diamonds i
shall throw them stone by stone in your
ancient teeth i will make songs against
your howling every black note will be
shimmering & beaded with poison

∽

it's a talent loving old men
their ancient scars so carefully
hidden under skin their great
anthologies of circumlocuted pain
their shining eyes their belly's
aching for new blood & i loved
you for wanting along this dark
knife's edge to go so much deeper
here on this edge of night with
me into the heart you said that
day of breaking

the year he was dying my father
put his house in order incorporated
his farm signed over the family
business to his only son before he
died my father tried to make sure
his daughters were saved confronted
each one about the state of her
soul i looked away while he prayed
like Daedalus with his mother at
the slow brown Red carrying its mud
past the hospital window stiffnecked
to the end before he died my father
put his house in order his acred
mansions & dreamed a garden for his
grave asked for flowers when he died
instead of the Bible plan

꿍

(for Rosie & for Esther Warkov)

the grandfathers she said are
falling everywhere & mine i know
fell long ago in the icing pink
car outside the church into open
mouthed oblivion his red leather
cheeks slowly fading to yellow so
why do i still see men with beards
& ladders dangling halfway in the
sky jesus hung as usual on every
available wall whatever happened
to our ballerina skirts & the
lipstick we exchanged on birthdays
the blanket you imagined made of
rose petals by an ancient you said
& powerful goddess the bed made of
grass & leaves & slightly hidden
among trees

4. hear them whispering

i wish the sky was still pasted on
to the ceiling the floor of God's
heaven i wish the stars were really
made of tin foil sliding at night
into dark earth under my bed i want
angels in cellophane surrounding my
head i want the old jesus with his
tin lantern & his sheep knocking
knocking at my wooden door i want
crashing alone into this black river
someone beside me the old old clutch
still at my soul

~⑤

mother why didn't you tell me this
how everything in the middle of life
becomes its opposite & all the signs
turn unreadable every direction a
dead end why didn't you tell me about
the belly's trembling just when you
need strength how the brain turns to
mush when it most needs to be clear
when you promised us passion & warned
us about boys why didn't you tell
about the body's great emptiness its
wanting the void the tight ache of
heart's muscle in the middle of night
the shaking of knees

trying to climb to you here
in the present i keep slipping
back you can't make anything
disappear all the horizontal
theories in the world can't
make the distance between us
less round the direction toward
you less up & down i look at
my hand in the water trailing
a lake remember how we once
skimmed these shining surfaces
hair to the wind now every
thought of you drops like a
stone every remembered desire
whispers death

how come there were all those stories
of the brother who made it in & the
brother who didn't i thought this was
a poem about love but it isn't it's
a poem about hate about being left out
in the cold it's a poem about sisters
my sister you the question is which of
us is the one that's out & which of us
in do you remember the dream was it
yours or mine in which one of us had
to die there wasn't room for us both
oh sister of mine whose name begins
with roses let there be room in this
mother's house for many mansions let's
make paths in this garden for two

❧

hear them whispering mother my unborn
children crying their sorrow without a
name why don't you love me why am i bad
how will i ever hold them all i need a
dozen arms a hundred breasts i need a
thousand love songs mother a lap as big
as earth

❧

(for my mother)

who would have thought all this time
you were the hula dancer the Hawaiian
girl our lady of flowers tossing gold
coins to strangers on street corners
scattering embroidered roses over
Los Angeles in winter forgetting
grandchildren garden house who could
have known behind your ancient women's
smile such glinting of teeth such
terrific abandon under dark empty
Pennsylvania skies the hot secret fire
of your pressed lips

❧

i wanted so much to be earth
mother for you holding together
your chaos in long blonde arms
rooting your severed pain in
wheatfield steadiness keeping
my promise like Mennonite grain
i wanted so much to be straight
& true & somehow miraculous for
you holding me at night my belly
full of tears it is you who keeps
the worlds from flying apart your
lips on my skin speak the dark
truth i am still lost i am scared
i am crazy wanting so much love
the lake & trees miracle of you

୶

you think if you say the right
words the jagged pieces will fit
you think a true sentence will
wrap itself around your red wound
like a fist if you wait long enough
she will rise from her charred bones
singing when did a single gut
wrenching sound ever escape its own
dark when we sat on the verandah
that night sorting our lives did we
hear the world's sobbing next door
our talk gathering like smoke &
a great hole in the floor

*in memory of Agnes Delaney who died
in a house fire on October 15, 1986

because she is not here i will
hold myself in my arms stroke
the emptiness in my belly with
unseeing hands rock my unspoken
grief back & forth back & forth
guide me safely through the night
my own mother knowing the world's
pain so finally so late from
inside a small baby's tenderness
singing my own sleep

seeing the world feelingly
like the blind man in my
bones i have come slowly
to this place by the river
long after you i have given
my eyes to the wind these
watery diamonds i have
given away all my words
hold me my sweet on this
flat chested earth with its
wild shining surfaces let
me weep one last time
for old kings while you
cover my bare limbs with
your wanting make the light
sing

~๑

i want you to know who are so
willing to wait so long i am
coming i am coming here beside
you in this red curtained room
through slaughter to your black
haired warmth somewhere inside
me the twisted little dwarf
juggling coins listens to your
voice & its echo a naked woman
with full breasts kneels before
living water drinks in darkness
your hot hungry love waits like
you for a new tender flowering

looking forward looking back

like jumping off a cliff the lip of the mountain
into the roiling volcano below & find there among
the lit up bleached bones & smoke & ash a narrow
opening through solid stone into another world
expanding rapidly into rooms & more rooms filled
with laughter & feasting & song the transformed
heart of our troubled mixed up culture(s) coming
to fruit

Thirty Years of Questions: An Afterword to Di Brandt's *questions i asked my mother*
by Tanis MacDonald

When Di Brandt visited Wilfrid Laurier University in 2009, she gave a short talk about her collection of essays, *Wider Boundaries of Daring: The Modernist Impulse in Canadian Women's Poetry*, and read some new poems that would later be included in her next book of poetry, *Walking to Mojácar*. During the course of the talk, she was kind enough to take questions, and students had many prepared for her: about writing, about poetry in Canada, about Mennonite culture. When there was time for only one more question, the students were silent, so I asked the question I had been thinking about. I asked Di to choose her "most feminist poem" to read; I had brought copies of all of her poetry books so she could select a poem from any of them. I added that she could choose any definition of feminist that she wanted, and that as our guest, she could read the poem free from the need to explain or discuss.

It's hard to say what I expected: maybe an ecofeminist poem from her Griffin Poetry Prize–nominated collection *Now You Care*, or a poem about peace from *Jerusalem, beloved*. Or maybe she would say that she had already read it that day—from her new manuscript. Instead, Di looked at me with an expression that is difficult to describe, except I will. Di shot me a look that was full of asperity and courage and sly humour. She shot me a look that moved the molecules around my face; she shot me a look that I am still feeling somewhere behind my eyes. Then she reached over to the pile of her books, picked up the one with a bright yellow cover, turned to a page near the beginning and began reading:

> my mother found herself one late summer
> afternoon lying in grass under the wild
> yellow plum tree jewelled with sunlight

The book with the bright yellow cover was Di's first collection of poems, *questions i asked my mother*, published by Turnstone Press in 1987. The poem she chose is an homage to a woman's moment spent imagining other worlds in a life crammed full of the practical demands of motherhood and farm life. The phrase "my mother found herself" puns on the feminist consciousness-raising groups of the 1970s as much as it gestures to a more meditative and sensual experience of lying beneath a tree on a summer day, an Edenic activity that would have been unusual for hard-working Mennonite women with several children and the endless daily chores that a working farm dictates. In this poem, the hard-working woman becomes the fallen blossoms, the rotting fruit beneath the tree, and the garden itself. Rising up from that old metaphor is her visionary self, her feminine spirit. My family isn't Mennonite, though Di and I have some geographic roots in common; my parents were both raised in rural communities in southern Manitoba, not far from the North Dakota border and close to the communities of Reinland where Di grew up, and to Winkler, where she went to high school. So for me, her choice of this poem—rural, maternal, historical, agrarian, and still rooted in materialist feminism—was both striking in its domesticity and inevitable in its politics, and it reminded me, sharply, of the subversiveness of Di's first book: how it leapt straight from a sixteenth-century separatist Mennonite community into late twentieth-century women's writing, drawing with it a series of revelations about silence and speech in the dynamics of growing up female in a traditional community. For many people who lived in Manitoba, the Mennonites were the people we knew as neighbours but could not really know because of their separate communities. The surprise of these poems, with Di's sometimes breathless, sometimes bawdy, sometimes furious voice, was the way the book offered not only a window onto resistance in female Mennonite lives, but also a look at women's speech outside of the traditional community, holding the mirror up to what it meant to be female and silenced anywhere in the world.

In some ways, it could be said that the shock waves set off by *questions i asked my mother* are still reverberating through the Canadian Mennonite community. To say that the book upset more than a few patriarchal traditionalists who benefitted from and sought to perpetuate female silence would be an understatement. Looking back nearly thirty years later, it is easy to forget the kind of stir this book created when it was first published as part of a wave of Mennonite writing and women's writing that burst onto the scene in Manitoba, reaching well across the country. One of the first biographies I ever read about Di declared that she "was still recovering from the scandal of being a Mennonite woman writer." Certainly the publication of *questions* reverberated through traditional Mennonite communities like the striking of a forbidden gong, as readers discovered that the book's poetic persona addresses subjects like family violence, female speech, segregated communities, and a triumvirate of sex, shame, and sin, and goes on to question authority in the various shapes of father, family, husband, community, culture, religion and God.

The book cost its author a lot, as well; censorious responses came from various parts of the Mennonite community, including Di's home community, and not all of that acrimony has faded with time. Beginning with *questions i asked my mother*, and continuing with her second book of poetry, *Agnes in the sky* (1990), and in recent essays in her collection *So this is the world and here I am in it* (2007) and elsewhere, Di's writing grapples with how the love for community, with its "stern, proud, humble, retrograde, free-spirited heritage" and utopian, revisionary intentions ("*Je jelieda*" 107), is complicated by the frustrations met by a thinking, curious woman speaking in the postmodern mode.

It is the act of questioning that is significant in this book; the thread of defiance that weaves through this collection is accompanied by love for father, mother, sister, friends, children, partner, and nature in all her forms. The scandal of *questions i asked my mother* can be found—at least in part—in how Di examines the many ways that love and anger live so near to each other in daily life and what happens when each is denied expression. Not for nothing does the mother sigh: "you're asking me something / i can't tell you she said now help me punch down the dough" in the poem from which the collection takes its title. What rises up, what gets punched down, and how can we live with the rules that govern which is allowed and which is not? And more radically, how can we find our way to greater freedom, more breathing room, to a place where women can speak—and write—more freely?

Context is important, whether you are reading *questions i asked my mother* for the first time or rereading after a number of years. Di's membership in the feminist writing group *hiatus* was a major influence, as she notes in her 1987 interview with Janice Williamson: "I found myself in this room with other young women who were as tentative and hesitant about their vision of the world as I was; they dared to call themselves writers and think of themselves as real writers in the world, and for me that was a very crucial contact" (40). Reading Daphne Marlatt's poetry was also influential for Di, especially as she wrestled with the problem of claiming space to speak on the page, admiring the way Marlatt's poetry was "pushing against the dark, not knowing where the words, the spirit, breath, the *nothing* in them, would take her" (Brandt, "Literary Foremothers" 14).

Winnipeg in the mid-1980s saw heady intersections of multiculturalism and feminism and civil rights activities. Across the country, First Nations writers like Tomson Highway and Jeannette Armstrong were demonstrating that it was possible to bring sacred oral sensibilities into contemporary writing. The first national Canadian women's literary conference Women and Words, which Di attended, was held at UBC in Vancouver in 1983 and exerted a huge generative influence on Canadian women's writing. International Canadian Studies programs were flourishing, helping to bring international interest and awareness to new Canadian writers. Winnipeg had also gained strong cosmopolitan and activist voices in the 1970s, voices that included that of Dorothy Livesay when she returned to the city of her childhood, after many years abroad, to serve as writer-in-residence at the University of Manitoba. In 1975, Livesay founded the national literary magazine *Contemporary Verse 2*, exerting a strong feminist poetic influence on Winnipeg's literary scene. Writer and scholar Robert Kroetsch moved back to Canada in 1978 from upper New York State to begin teaching at the University of Manitoba, bringing his generosity for new writers and a passion for Prairie literature.

Into this mixture of culture, politics, and art, the effect of Mennonite-inflected poetry on the burgeoning milieu of Manitoban literary culture was profound; Turnstone Press co-founder David Arnason notes that poetry granted many writers from Mennonite backgrounds a chance to speak their truth against tradition, and Turnstone's role in publishing these writers has been one of the press's proudest legacies. While many critics think of Rudy Wiebe's 1962 novel *Peace Shall Destroy Many* as the breakout book of Mennonite literature, that book, and the criticism with which it was met by the Mennonite community, had a dual effect: Canadian readers became aware of some aspects of Mennonite culture through the novel, but the book's controversy made the idea of being a Mennonite writer daunting. As Arnason says in his paper about Turnstone's history of publishing Mennonite writers, "Rudy's example silenced writers at that point in the emergence of the literature, rather than getting them to speak" (215). But poetry, Arnason notes, was the genre of hope for young Mennonite writers: "a way of coming to talk about themselves and to write" (215).

The originating poets were Patrick Friesen, Victor Enns, Audrey Thiessen and Di Brandt. All were active in creating the "new Mennonite" literary oeuvre, and simultaneously, the social context for its reception, by organizing poetry readings and professional writing groups, serving as poetry editors for literary magazines, and giving workshops, interviews and guest lectures. Poetry could access the oral speech rhythms of Mennonite traditionalism while at the same time wrestling with the displacements and disjunctions of the postmodern world. Together, these poets created a performative literary community; they had grown up during the upheavals of 1960s and 1970s counterculture, and—no surprise—they had their own hard-won perspectives on the ways and means of "cultural revolution." Courage and innovation were the media of exchange between the new Mennonite poets. Patrick Friesen's publications with Turnstone Press—especially *The Shunning* (1980) and *unearthly horses* (1984)—with their passionate critiques of Mennonite patriarchy, encouraged Di to publish her own culturally explosive *questions i asked my mother*; Friesen's 1987 collection *Flicker and Hawk*, as David Arnason notes, showed a new ease with the long sonorous line he inherited from hearing Di's charged poetic rhythms. This energetic local poetry scene had a lasting impact on Manitoban, Canadian, and ultimately, international literary and cultural life, in Mennonite circles and beyond.

A few years after *questions i asked my mother* was published, Di initiated a special Mennonite Writing issue of *Prairie Fire* magazine, where she was poetry editor, inviting scholar Hildi Froese Tiessen to guest-edit the issue and bring some academic attention to the burgeoning literary movement. Tiessen did, and the issue came out in 1990. Tiessen subsequently organized the first Mennonite/s Writing conference at the University of Waterloo in 1990, focusing on the emerging importance of the Winnipeg poets and the influence of Turnstone Press. Other such conferences followed in church-based Mennonite colleges in the United States, and in the Mennonite Studies program at the University of Winnipeg, with the aim of confronting the challenges that the new Mennonite writing posed for a traditionalist community in flux. In 2003, American poet and critic Ann Hostetler published *A Capella*, the first North American anthology of Mennonite poetry, a book that prominently featured Winnipeg writers in an international Mennonite context. Mennonite literature became a critical category as well as a cultural practice, intersecting with other categories of production and reception—Winnipeg literature, Prairie literature, feminist literature, postmodern literature, Canadian literature, and world literature: energetic and far-reaching, the multi-armed result of a variety of influences and confluences. This was the multi-faceted literary world that proceeded directly from the work of *questions i asked my mother* and its young author, and her collaborating colleagues of the day.

For a first book of poems, *questions i asked my mother* is an astonishing achievement and critical success, written with a breathless yet sure voice, leaping from one precarious exclamation to another. It seems boldly prescient when I read it now, but it is also a book of extreme vulnerability, and it is hard to say which was (and is) more scandalous: the poet's voice that challenges the "clearcut invisible lines of / propriety which could not be argued or discussed" in the poem "shades of sin," or the voice that argues Biblical interpretation with her father through "clenched teeth" in "but what do you think my father says," or the heartbroken voice speaking from "this huge empty tear in the / chest" in the poem beginning "i hate desire the hot animal itch." The book was first published in the heady days when French feminist theory was finding its feet in some of our scholarly institutions, when studies on mother-daughter kinship were not yet a staple of feminist dissertations. No wonder Magdalene Redekop wrote for the back cover of *questions i asked my mother*: "Read these poems and you will hear a Mennonite Eve stealing some breath for herself." Feminist icon and poet Daphne Marlatt also noted Di's "considerable poetic verve (and nerve) at the very heart of the spiritual-sexual nexus." Fifteen years later, in 2003, as I heard Canadian literary critics outside of Manitoba talk about the way that Toews's *A Complicated Kindness* had blown the lid off of Mennonite life in Canada, I remembered (as Miriam herself has frequently acknowledged, most recently during her book tour for *All My Puny Sorrows*) that Di had done it first. I think something similar whenever I hear people speaking about the American Mennonite Julia Spicher Kasdorf's *Sleeping Preacher* (1992), which includes a poem titled "What I Learned From My Mother," and praising the book for its groundbreaking exploration of the female body in Mennonite poetry. Kasdorf and Toews are both excellent and courageous writers, and I will always argue for reading subversive feminist books, but to give literary historical credit where credit is due, we must acknowledge that *questions i asked my mother* came first in a way that was encouragingly influential and generative for both of these women and for women writers from all kinds of backgrounds around the world.

David Arnason, who would later become Di's doctoral dissertation supervisor at the University of Manitoba, has spoken of the manuscript submission process for *questions i asked my mother* as one in which the publishers at Turnstone Press "begged" Di to submit the manuscript to them. He recalls: "She in fact did submit it once, and then seized it the day after and took it back; it took nearly a year before we got it back again" (Arnason 221). While it is safe to say that many first-time authors are anxious prior to publication, this was something more than just jitters. Not every first-time author takes on the authority of a culture, a community, and a religious tradition; not every first-time author makes herself as vulnerable as Di does in acknowledging in herself "the rebel traitor thief / the one who asked too many questions" ("foreword"). Di was not surprised by the hostile response she received from much of the North American Mennonite community for the ways she spoke of the separatist community to outsiders, challenging her father's generation of men and their authoritative language and, with considerable audacity, daring to reclaim her past, "living my inheritance on this black earth" on her own terms ("foreword').

She was, however, pleasantly surprised to receive an "intense and warm" response from certain Mennonite women's groups, such as the female audience members who heard her read at the Swiss-Mennonite Bicentennial Celebration in Toronto in 1986, women who also confirmed her visibility by approaching her and saying, in a whisper, "You're saying all this for me. This is also my experience, but I'm too scared to say it" (Brandt qtd. in Williamson 33–34). In 1989, a few years after the publication of *questions i asked my mother*, Di noted in an address at the University of Trier in Germany: "What the new Mennonite poetry does is to bring the story back home, back to earth, where hurt is really hurt, and death is really death and desire is really and truly desire" ("Dancing" 36).

In the world of Canadian literature, the publication of *questions i asked my mother* made readers across the country sit up and take notice, garnering many supportive reviews. John Oughton, in the March 1988 issue of *Books in Canada*, reviewed it alongside two new books by established poets Stephen Scobie and Henry Kreisel, and called Di's first book "surrealistic and visionary," as well as a book that offered "the viewpoint of a sensual yet sceptical feminist." Impressively, Oughton began his review with an acknowledgement of its power: "Two words about this book: buy it" (33). The book was widely reviewed by other respected literary magazines, by Karen Ruttan in *Poetry Canada Review*, by Rosalind Conway in the scholarly journal *Canadian Literature*, and by Ralph Friesen in *Border Crossings*. Nadine McInnis, reviewing in *Journal of Canadian Poetry*, calls *questions i asked my mother* "an unusual first book in the fullness of its vision" and calls Di "a gifted, feminist writer interested in stretching poetic form and language" (36). McInnis takes special care to point out that the book foregrounds the risks that Di had taken to write it, and notes that "it is rare to find such perfect twinning of theme and technique, so seemingly effortless, integrated as mirror images" (33). She concludes: "Stories matter; poetry shakes foundations. These new structures are soundly, lovingly constructed" (McInnis 36).

The book also received a good deal of attention from mainstream media both in Canada and in the UK, and Di appeared in numerous radio and television features across the country, discussing the book's generation and its impact. Robert Quickenden's review of *questions i asked my mother* in the *Winnipeg Free Press* noted the book's aim "to find a public voice that is still true to private experience" with "an awareness that our prisons often define our freedom." The book also attracted much attention in the professional literary community, receiving the Gerald Lampert Award for "best first book of poetry in Canada" from the League of Canadian Poets, as well as nominations for bot the Governor General's Award for Poetry and the prestigious Dillons Commonwealth Poetry Prize in the UK. All this professional attention was accompanied by ardent fan mail to the author from readers around the world, a lot of it for the first few years following the book's publication, and some ever since.

In the ensuing years, scholarly response to *questions i asked my mother* has noted that Di's feminist transgression begins with the family, but extends to an address of hidden female realities and mounts a challenge to patriarchal language. Grace Kehler, in the earliest of these critical articles, "Stealing the Word(s): The Subversion of Monologic Language in Di Brandt's *questions i asked my mother*," notes that Di "re-writes and re-constructs her problematic heritage that she cannot entirely embrace or disavow" (25). Appearing in *Open Letter* in the spring of 1995, Kehler's article focuses on the book's "Promethean endeavour," an apt allusion to the Greek myth about the theft of fire from the gods, and observes that the tensions of inclusion and exclusion in Di's poetry make it impossible to "insist on one epistemological model as truth and ignore its reductiveness" (27). Sheldon Fisher's 1996 article regards the book as "a particularly useful matrix" in which to study mother-daughter dialogue, a project that he identifies as being simultaneously ancient and part of the reclaiming of maternal experience in the feminist discourse of the 1980s and 1990s (32). In this study, *questions i asked my mother* appears as a text that captures the "deep, painful disappointment" of a daughter abandoned by the mother before seeking and speaking with "an enlightened mother-voice" in later collections (Fisher 33).

Marie Carrière, in her 2002 study *Writing in the Feminine in*

French and English Canada: A Question of Ethics, includes *questions i asked my mother* in a "Mothers and Daughters" section, and begins by examining the book's act of interrogation. "Brandt's first and most controversial work ... describes a struggle for voice and for authorship" notes Carrière, in which the feminist author adopts the strategy of "both subverting and commemorating the master narrative under scrutiny, before attempting to rewrite it" (73). Like Kehler, Carrière also finds the roots of Greek myths in the book, observing the strong pull of the Demeter-Persephone myth in the poems' renderings of Christian and linguistic experiences (76). Di notes in the "foreword" to the text that her speaking persona is considered "questionable" because of the resistance she mounts by asking questions, implying, at least in part, a kind of perpetual cycle familiar in feminism: that curiosity and intelligence, especially in a woman, is always a questionable position. For Carrière, the text enacts this kind of rhetorical turnabout as "the risk, difficulty, and cost for the female writer who breaks away from the rules, the official histories, and even the community which have constituted her, contained her, at times abused as well as protected her" (Carrière 74).

In the study of Canadian prairie, Mennonite and women's literature, Di's books have become staple texts, and her first book has drawn attention for its consideration of the mother-daughter relationship as fraught precisely because the mother does not (or cannot) answer the daughter's questions. Douglas Reimer, in his book *Surplus at the Border: Mennonite Writing in Canada,* notes that the title poem "questions i asked my mother" marks the start of a "heroic quest, with all the dangers and contest heroes face and manage" (118) to discover the undiscoverable, the answers to the daughter's questions; and Di carries on to reframe those questions about motherhood in her 1992 poetry collection, *mother, not mother.* Sharon Butala, in her 2005 book *Lilac Moon: Dreaming of the Real West,* notes the "major effect" that *questions i asked my mother* had "on Westerners... Or perhaps I should say, especially on women. It is profoundly feminist ... and the voice is so true, so pain-filled, so powerful in its effect that once read, it cannot be forgotten" (Butala 189). The book's setting is the Canadian prairies, but the book's appeal has been international; Di has travelled the world, giving readings and talks at conferences and festivals in many countries. Given the book's enduring and wide readership, we shouldn't think of *questions* as solely a Mennonite text, but rather as a quintessential prairie text of rebellion and renewal against many forces: patriarchal, cultural, linguistic, and literary.

Since the publication of *questions i asked my mother*, Di has published six other collections of poetry, including 2003's *Now You Care*, which was nominated for both Ontario's Trillium Prize for Best Book and for the prestigious Griffin Poetry Prize for the best book of Canadian poetry in that year. As a scholar, Di has published a book of literary criticism (*Wild Mother Dancing: Maternal Narrative in Canadian Literature*), two collections of essays (*Dancing Naked: Narrative Strategies for Writing across Centuries* in 1996 and *So this is the world & here I am in it* in 2007), and edited several more collections and special issues of scholarly and creative writing. (A complete list of Di's major works appears elsewhere in this book, though readers should know that there are more books in the works even as I write.) Di's collaborations with other writers and artists include *Watermelon Syrup: A Novel*, with Annie Jacobsen and Jane Finlay-Young; translations of her own poems into French and Spanish; the libretto for an opera, *Emily, the Way You Are*, about the life and work of Emily Carr, with composer Jana Skarecky; and the poetry/music project *Awakenings: In Four Voices* with the poetry of Dorothy Livesay, and composers Carol Ann Weaver and Rebecca Campbell.

In 2006, I wrote the introduction for Di's volume of selected works, *Speaking of Power,* published by Wilfrid Laurier University Press in their Laurier Poetry Series. Di's books have been reviewed widely and written about by Canadian scholars and writers other than those discussed earlier in this essay, scholars who are interested in her views of ecocriticism (Lousley, Hostetler), motherhood and feminist resistance (Boire, O'Reilly), as well as in studies positioning Di's work among women writers in Mennonite culture (Loewen, Redekop, Tefs, Tiessen), and in Canadian multicultural literature (Kamboureli). Grace Kehler has also written a thoughtful discussion about the turn away from the fatality of cultural martyrdom so central to Mennonite identity towards "a form of praise" in Di's poetry, "a paradoxical hymn of loving lament for the emergent community, whose broken beauties nonetheless bespeak the potentiality of revitalized inter-relations" (Kehler 2011, 170). These "broken beauties" have attracted national and international attention, including Liam Lacey's 1990 feature on Di in *The Globe and Mail*, and the scrutiny of critics from the United States (Hostetler, Gundy), as well as in Germany (Kuester, Löschnigg, Zirker,) and the translations of her poems by others into German, French, Spanish, Catalan, and Japanese; "non-resistance, or love Mennonite style" was translated into Czech for the journal *PLAV* in 2010.

Recent years have shown a new generation of scholars reading Di's early work, not surprising since it continues to be taught in universities throughout Canada. Robert Zacharias names Di as a mentor and foremother figure in his 2013 study *Rewriting the Break Event: Mennonites and Migration in Canadian Literature*. Natasha Wiebe's 2008 article "Mennocostal Musings: Poetic Inquiry and Performance in Narrative Research" parses her own reading of *questions i asked my mother* as initially shocked, then analytical about the book's satirical tone, and finally curious about how to use her own poetry as a similar mode of rebellion and revision from within a traditional culture.

Di has said that with *questions i asked my mother* she was challenging the official story of patriarchal authority and transgressing narrative in order to time travel from a traditionalist communal identity to a modern individuated one: "I was trying to write myself into the twentieth century" (qtd. in Williamson 48). The wry epigraph to the book, "some of this is autobiographical / & some of it is not," speaks to the kind of authorial leap she was making, one that encompasses many forms of truth-telling, plus the liberal application of hyperbole that always circles back to the authenticity of experience. The fifth annual international Mennonite/s Writing conference held at the University of Winnipeg in October 2009 included a bus tour of the literary "Mennonite country" of southern Manitoba, featuring a traditional Faspa dinner served in the Reinland Community Centre by the community, including members of Di's extended family, at which Di read from *questions i asked my mother* (Hostetler, "Letters Home"). Natasha Wiebe called that reading a "historic occasion" and I can only agree. While life is long and sometimes the process of truth and reconciliation—and forgiveness—takes even longer, to see evidence of a full circle scandal-to-homecoming arc for a book that has been so daring is evidence of the value of speaking.

When I teach poems from *questions i ask my mother,* two things always happen, regular as clockwork, which is not to say that such things are banal, only that the impact of Di's early work is still being felt by the texting generation. The first thing that always happens is that students will say with delight, "I didn't know you could do this with poetry/punctuation/the line/argument," so happy that Di's poetry gives them permission to read expansively and write while deciding how and why to exert their own pressures on language, to defy the rules as they have learned them and come back from the journey knowing more about creative disobedience and the laws of language. This is inevitably good for their critical thinking as well as their writing, and the results are evident. The other thing that happens is more individual and more private. A student, or maybe two or three, will approach me after the class and say privately but with a shocked recognition: "This is my story. I grew up in a tradition like this. This is the inside of my head." I know that other readers, outside the classroom and in other countries, have responded in similar ways. The traditions in question vary, but the result is the same. Reading *questions i asked my mother* remains a radical act.

Works Cited

Arnason, David. "A History of Turnstone Press." *Acts of Concealment: Mennonite/s Writing in Canada*. Ed. Hildi Froese Tiessen and Peter Hinchcliffe. Waterloo: University of Waterloo Press, 1992. 212–222. Print.

Boire, Gary. "Transparencies: Of Sexual Abuse, Ambivalence and Resistance." *Essays on Canadian Writing* 51–52. (1993/94): 211–232. Print.

Brandt, Di. "Dancing Naked: Narrative Strategies for Writing Across Centuries." *Dancing Naked: Narrative Strategies for Writing Across Centuries*. Stratford, ON: Mercury Press, 1996. 32–42. Print.

-----. "*Je jelieda, je vechieda*: Canadian Mennonite (Alter) Identifications." *So this is the world & here I am in it*. Edmonton: NeWest Press, 2007. 105–132. Print.

-----. "Literary Foremothers." *Dancing Naked*. 12–14. Print.

-----. "Neodporování zlému, aneb láska v mennonitském stylu." ("non-resistance, or love Mennonite style"). Trans. Miroslav Jindra. *PLAV* 7/8 (2010): 56–57. Print.

-----. Personal email to Tanis MacDonald. 17 March 2015.

-----. *questions i asked my mother*. Winnipeg: Turnstone Press, 1987. Print.

-----. "The sadness in this book is that I'm reaching for this story..." Interview with Janice Williamson. *Sounding Differences: Conversations with Seventeen Canadian Women Writers*. Ed. Williamson. Toronto: University of Toronto Press, 1993. 31–53. Print.

Butala, Sharon. *Lilac Moon: Dreaming of the Real West*. Toronto: HarperCollins, 2005. Print.

Carrière, Marie. "Questioning the Mother: Di Brandt." *Writing in the Feminine in French and English Canada: A Question of Ethics*. Toronto: University of Toronto Press, 2002. 72–84. Print.

Conway, Rosalind E. "Striking Earth." *Canadian Literature* 122–123 (1989): 278–279. Print.

Fisher, Sheldon. "Mother, Me, My Daughter: Feminism, Maternité, and the Poetry of Di Brandt." *Wascana Review* 31.1 (1996): 31–48. Print.

Friesen, Patrick. *Flicker and Hawk.* Winnipeg: Turnstone Press, 1987. Print.

-----. *The Shunning.* Winnipeg: Turnstone Press, 1980. Print.

-----. *unearthly horses.* Winnipeg: Turnstone Press, 1984. Print.

Friesen, Ralph. Review of *questions i asked my mother. Border Crossings* 7.2 (1988): 30–31. Print.

Gundy, Jeff. "New Maps of the Territories: On Mennonite Writing." *Georgia Review* 57.4 (2003). Print.

Hostetler, Ann, ed. *A Cappella: Mennonite Voices in Poetry.* Iowa City: University of Iowa Press, 2003. Print.

-----. "A Valediction Forbidding Excommunication: Ecopoetics and the Reparative Journey Home in Recent Work by Di Brandt." *Journal of Mennonite Studies* 28 (2010): 69–86. Print.

-----. "Letters Home: An Informal Report on Mennonite/s Writing: Manitoba and Beyond." *Journal of the Center for Mennonite Writing* 6 (2009). Web.

Kamboureli, Smaro. *Making a Difference: Canadian Multicultural Literature.* Toronto: Oxford University Press, 1996. Print.

Kasdorf, Julia Spicher. *Sleeping Preacher.* Pittsburgh: University of Pittsburgh Press, 1992. Print.

Kehler, Grace. "Representations of Melancholic Martyrdom in Canadian Mennonite Literature." *Journal of Mennonite Studies* 29 (2011): 167–185. Print.

-----. "Stealing the Word(s): The Subversion of Monologic Language in Di Brandt's *Questions i asked my mother." Open Letter* 9.2 (1995): 19–28. Print.

Kuester, Martin. "A Complicated Kindness: The Contribution of Mennonite Authors to Canadian Literature." Trans. Gerhard Reimer. *Journal of the Center for Mennonite Writing* 3.2 (2011). Web.

-----. "Nationality and Belonging in Mennonite Women's Writing: Di Brandt's Poetry and Criticism." *Her Na-rra-tion: Women's Narratives of the Canadian Nation.* Eds. Françoise Lejeune and Charlotte Sturgess. Nantes: CRINI/CEC Université de Nantes, 2009. 129–139. Print.

Loewen, Harry. "Leaving Home: Canadian Mennonite Literature in the 1980s." *Canadian Review of Comparative Literature: Revue Canadienne de littérature comparée* (1989): 687–691. Print.

Löschnigg, Maria. "NAFTA we worship you: Conservationism and the Critique of Economic Liberalism in Twenty-First Century Canadian Poetry." *Zeitschrift für Kanada-Studien* 34 (2014): 28–45. Print.

-----. "Words 'bubbling up from the belly': On Di Brandt's Poetic Work." *Literatur in Wissenschaft und Unterricht* 37.2 (2004): 133–157. Print.

Lousley, Cheryl. "Home on the Prairie: A Feminist and Postcolonial Reading of Sharon Butala, Di Brandt, and Joy Kogawa." *ISLE: Interdisciplinary Studies in Literature and Environment* 8.2 (2001): 71–95. Print.

McInnis, Nadine. Review of *questions i asked my mother. Journal of Canadian Poetry* 4 (1987): 32–36. Print.

O'Reilly, Andrea. "Stories to Live By: Maternal Literatures and Motherhood Studies." *Textual Mothers, Maternal Texts: Motherhood in Contemporary Women's Literatures.* Ed. Elizabeth Podnieks and Andrea O'Reilly. Waterloo, ON: Wilfrid Laurier University Press, 2010. 367–373. Print.

Oughton, John. "New Voices, Old Ballads." *Books in Canada* 17.2 (1988): 33–34. Print.

Quickenden, Robert. "Glimpses of a closed world." *Winnipeg Free Press.* 12 March 1988. Print.

Prairie Fire. "New Mennonite Writing" issue. Ed. Hildi Froese Tiessen. 2.2 (1990). Print.

Redekop, Magdalene. "The Pickling of the Mennonite Madonna." *Acts of Concealment: Mennonite/s Writing in Canada.* Ed. Hildi Froese Tiessen and Peter Hinchcliffe. Waterloo: University of Waterloo Press, 1992. 100–128. Print.

Reimer, Douglas. "Father, Mother and Mennonite Me: Di Brandt and the Overthrow of the Mother." *Surplus at the Border: Mennonite Writing in Canada*. Winnipeg: Turnstone Press, 2002. 99—132. Print.

Ruttan, Karen. Review of *questions i asked my mother*. *Poetry Canada Review* 10.1 (1989): 5—9. Print.

Tefs, Wayne. "Rage in Some Recent Mennonite Poetry." *Acts of Concealment: Mennonite/s Writing in Canada*. Ed. Hildi Froese Tiessen and Peter Hinchcliffe. Waterloo: University of Waterloo Press, 1992. 193–205. Print.

Tiessen, Hildi Froese. "Mother Tongue as Shibboleth in the Literature of Canadian Mennonites." *Studies in Canadian Literature* 13.2 (1988). 175–183. Print.

Toews, Miriam. *A Complicated Kindness*. Toronto: Vintage Canada, 2003. Print.

Wiebe, Natasha G. "Mennocostal Musings: Poetic Inquiry and Performance in Narrative Research." *Forum: Qualitative Social Research* 9.2 (2008). Web.

Wiebe, Rudy. *Peace Shall Destroy Many*. 1962. Toronto: Vintage Canada, 2001. Print.

Zacharias, Robert. *Rewriting the Break Event: Mennonites and Migration in Canadian Literature*. Winnipeg: University of Manitoba Press, 2013. Print.

Zirker, Herbert. *Selected Essays in English Literatures, British and Canadian: Jonathan Swift, John Fowles, Margaret Laurence, Margaret Atwood, Di Brandt & Dennis Cooley*. Frankfurt: Peter Lang, 2002. Print.

Bibliography of Major Works

Poetry

questions i asked my mother. Winnipeg: Turnstone Press, 1987.

Agnes in the sky. Winnipeg: Turnstone Press, 1990.

mother, not mother. Toronto: Mercury Press, 1992.

Jerusalem, beloved. Winnipeg: Turnstone Press, 1995.

Now You Care. Toronto: Coach House Press, 2003.

Speaking of Power: The Selected Poetry of Di Brandt. Ed. with intro. by Tanis MacDonald. Laurier Poetry Series. Waterloo, ON: Wilfrid Laurier University Press, 2006.

Walking to Mojácar. With French and Spanish translations by Charles Leblanc and Ari Belathar. Winnipeg: Turnstone Press, 2010.

SHE: Poems inspired by Laozi's Dao De Jing. With ink drawings by Lin Xu. Brandon, MB: Radish Press, 2012.

Literary and Multimedia Collaborations

Awakenings: In Four Voices. Poetry by Di Brandt and Dorothy Livesay, music by Carol Ann Weaver and Rebecca Campbell. CD recording, 2003.

Emily, the Way You Are. With composer Jana Skarecky. Chamber opera. 2011.

Watermelon Syrup: A Novel. With Annie Jacobsen and Jane Finlay-Young. Waterloo, ON: Wilfrid Laurier University Press, 2011.

Coyotes do not carry her away. With composer Kenneth Nichols. Song cycle. 2012.

Granada. With composer Kenneth Nichols. Song cycle. 2013.

Creative and Critical Essay Collections

Wild Mother Dancing: Maternal Narrative in Canadian Literature. Winnipeg: University of Manitoba, 1993.

Dancing Naked: Narrative Strategies for Writing Across Centuries. Toronto: Mercury Press, 1996.

So this is the world & here I am in it. Writer as Critic series. Ed. Smaro Kamboureli. Edmonton: NeWest Press, 2007.

Edited Anthologies

Re:Generations: Canadian Women Poets in Conversation. Ed. with Barbara Godard. Windsor, ON: Black Moss Press, 2006.

Wider Boundaries of Daring: The Modernist Impulse in Canadian Writing. Ed. with Barbara Godard. Waterloo, ON: Wilfrid Laurier University Press, 2011.